This study was supported by funds from the U. S. Department
of Housing and Urban Development. The views expressed
herein are those of the authors and do not necessarily represent
those of either The Urban Institute or the U. S. Department of
Housing and Urban Development.

Available from:

Publications Office
The Urban Institute
2100 M Street, N.W.
Washington, D.C. 20037

List price: $1.95
Refer to URI-16000 When Ordering

UI 201- 2
LC 72-95475

Contents

Exhibits

Acknowledgments

George Wickstrom, Metropolitan Washington Council of Governments, provided helpful suggestions at various stages of this work. Rhona Pavis of The Urban Institute provided much of the initial background research. The authors are also grateful to the following persons for their critiques and suggestions: George Bell, Council of State Governments; Donald J. Borut, International City Management Association; James Clark, D.C. Department of Highways; William Goodman, Carl Rappaport and James Sale, U.S. Department of Transportation; James Scott, Highway Research Board; Allen Schick, Brookings Institution; Richard Soberman, Centre for Urban and Community Studies, University of Toronto; and Peter Brown, Donald M. Fisk, Damian Kulash, Philip Schaenman, and Kenneth Webb of The Urban Institute.

Summary

Local officials cannot meet their transportation responsibilities adequately unless they know how well they are serving community needs. Unfortunately there are major gaps in the data that would answer this question in a fair and comprehensive manner. This publication attempts to help local governments overcome this deficiency.

An effectiveness measurement system is proposed. It emphasizes the quality of local transportation from the standpoint of the citizen-consumer.

The system begins with the formulation of major objectives of a local transportation system: ease of access to the places people want to go, convenience, travel time (reasonable speed), comfort, safety, economy, maintenance of a habitable environment, and satisfaction among citizens with the overall adequacy of the system.

One or more measures for each of these objectives is specified. For example, under "time," the travel time between major destinations and the duration of congestion would be calculated. Local officials are encouraged to review the objectives and measures carefully, modifying them when appropriate because of local needs and circumstances.

The suggested measures are intended to apply to all modes of transportation, not, for instance, to automobiles or bus service alone. But if a community becomes particularly concerned about a single type of transportation, the measures can be focused separately on that one mode.

The measurement system aims to assess the general quality of transportation within local jurisdictions. Equally important, it aims to throw light on transportation for distinct segments of the community— different neighborhoods, the rich and the poor, the young and the old, those with autos, and those who rely on public transportation.

A major part of this report describes procedures whereby data may be collected for each of the effectiveness measures. The recommended data-gathering techniques include field measurements, the use of mapping to analyze public transit in relation to population distribution, and citizen surveys. Annual collection of data and preparation of measurements are urged.

Annual costs of carrying out the proposed measurement system are estimated at about $37,500 for cities of 150,000 and about $93,000 for cities of 750,000. This would be in addition to current costs of statistical operations. The outlay of funds for implementing the system can be reduced, sub-stantially in some cases, by using present municipal staff, applying for federal funding, sharing costs and operations with other local agencies (such as regional transportation planning bodies), and cooperating with local transit firms.

The measurement system is not recommended for its own sake. No matter how well it is devised and carried out, no matter how well it is financed and staffed, and no matter how sophisticated the analysis of data, the value of the system ultimately rests on its utilization by local officials. By com-paring the measurements over time and among different seg-ments of the community, officials may identify problem areas, trends, and progress (or lack of progress). The measurement system may not tell what should be done but will point to the areas that require further detailed investigations. The system is expected to help officials reach improved decisions on the level of local spending for transportation, on the way those funds are expended, on the kinds of regulations needed, and on the overall policies pursued.

The techniques set forth apply generally to municipalities, urban counties, and metropolitan transportation agencies whose jurisdictions have 50,000 or more people. The measurement system has not yet been field tested. However, it is hoped that these tentative findings will be useful to local governments that are attempting to devise better measurements and will also help stimulate interest in improved measurement practices.

I. Introduction and Scope

Transportation has many facets. The emphasis of this publication is on *local* transportation— intracity or intracounty— and on the movement of *people* rather than of goods.

Current transportation measures (as discussed in Chapter II) generally fail to reflect the effectiveness of transportation systems from the citizens' perspective. This information gap impairs the ability of officials to judge present conditions or to arrive at sound decisions on transportation changes.

Because of the local emphasis, the modes of transportation of most interest in this work are automobiles, buses, taxis, rapid rail, and, to a limited extent, walking. The concern is with the way people get back and forth from local destinations, between their homes and their places of employment, recreation, and shopping.

In devising the data collection procedures (described in detail in Chapter IV), the aim was to produce methods that are practical and economic for local governments. In some cases, the need for new data seems imperative. Whenever possible, the measurement system calls for the use of data that are already available.

Few issues create more civic tension than disparities in public service — with some citizens receiving a high quality of service while others are relatively neglected. Officials typically have not had many ways to get a clear perspective of the service levels provided to different subgroups in their communities. This work seeks to correct this in the field of transportation by giving considerable attention to the quality and variety of service available to different population segments within a jurisdiction. Major residential neighborhoods are to be measured separately. Special attention is given to the elderly, young and others who do not have access to automobile transportation and who therefore must rely heavily on public transit. (Clientele groups are discussed further in Chapter V.)

1

Major uses of the proposed measurement system include the following:

> To indicate the effectiveness of transportation services currently available to the jurisdiction as a whole and to specific socio-economic and geographic segments.

> To provide baseline data. As the data are collected annually over time, the community's progress toward improving transportation services can be measured.

> To help identify existing transportation problems.

> To help analyze and evaluate proposed and experimental programs.

The measurement system is not set forth as a remedy for local transportation difficulties. It is designed to pinpoint what the conditions are, but it will not necessarily explain why these conditions exist or what programs should be undertaken to deal with them. Major transportation solutions often require detailed analysis and evaluation. The construction of a new highway system, for instance, affects a complex set of issues and proper planning would entail in-depth studies of anticipated impacts on the community's economy, land use pattern, and residential movements as well as on traffic conditions.

The report encourages the use of not just one measure, but rather a set of a dozen effectiveness measures. Each focuses on an important segment of service quality. Yet no single measure alone suffices for a comprehensive picture of local transportation service. Decision makers often tend to concentrate on the beneficial aspects of a proposal without explicitly weighing potential negative side effects. For example, introducing bus service in a residential neighborhood may improve service to persons along the route but, at the same time, cause noise and fumes which disturb other residents. Improving service according to one or a few measures can result in poorer performance on other measures. If, as frequently happens, one aspect of service must be sacrificed at the expense of another, this should not be a matter of accident but should result from a deliberate policy decision related to local priorities. Thus, while all measures may not pertain directly to every decision, each should be considered, at least briefly, to identify the various ways citizens may be affected by changes in transportation services.

As noted in the Summary, the data collection procedures have not yet been field tested and are neither detailed nor definitive for operating purposes. However, the general approach has proved useful for other local services such as recreation and solid waste collection.[1] The authors hope that their tentative conclusions will assist local government and regional planning bodies as they attempt to improve their assessments of transportation service.

---

1. Previous publications from this series of studies are *Measuring the Effectiveness of Local Government Services: Solid Waste Collection*, 1970, *Measuring the Effectiveness of Local Government Services: Recreation*, 1971, and *How Clean Is Our City?* 1972.

II. Current Measurement Practices

Of all public services in urban areas, transportation has received the most attention from professionals and academics. Government at all levels, transportation firms, and public interest organizations develop and disseminate a wide variety of transportation data and analytical techniques. As a basis for this report, we reviewed the transportation measurement techniques currently utilized by local governments or proposed in transportation literature.

The statistics usually available to local governments include descriptive information on the transportation system, such as miles of roadway, number of vehicles, seating capacities of public transit modes, yards of road surface constructed, number of street signs installed, man-years of maintenance effort, and traffic volume on various routes.

Local government traffic departments also regularly measure traffic volume on local and arterial streets. In its simplest form, traffic volume is counted for a period of time, such as twenty-four hours. More detailed cordon counts are also sometimes conducted to measure the number, type, and occupancy of vehicles entering or leaving a city. Public transit agencies monitor passenger volumes on transit lines, especially when a change of schedule or route is contemplated.

Usually local governments and transit agencies regularly collect information on transportation-related accidents, injuries, and fatalities. Official schedules and routes of public transit generally are available from transit firms. Some firms also monitor factors which affect user comfort, such as cleanliness and noise of vehicles, but seldom do the governments monitor such information.

Some cities measure the speed of traffic flow on major

5

arterials during peak travel periods. These data may be displayed on maps that show the distance it is possible to travel from a central point in various lengths of time. Travel time measurements may also be made for non-central trips, but this is not a common practice among cities.

Most measurements of travel time, traffic volume, and congestion are conducted in connection with specific proposed changes, for example, to compare congestion before and after the addition of a left-turn lane. Infrequent collection of such data does not enable them to be used for systematic comparisons over time.

Some metropolitan areas have access to increasingly comprehensive information on travel patterns as well as traveler behavior and mode preferences. Postcard or at-home surveys are conducted occasionally, but seldom on a regular basis, to ascertain attitudes of citizens toward available or proposed transportation services. Public transit surveys are apparently conducted infrequently, again, usually in connection with specific proposed changes.

To assess such factors as road surface condition, traffic control problems, and transit vehicle comfort, local governments generally rely on volunteered citizen complaints. A few state agencies occasionally measure road surface quality with mechanical devices, but local governments have not yet instituted this type of measurement.

The major deficiencies in current data collection practices for assessing the quality of local transportation services are:

1. Data are not collected on some important effects of the transportation system on the community and on

various neighborhoods and citizen subgroups. Among these neglected effects are accessibility, rider comfort, convenience, air and noise pollution, and general satisfaction as perceived by citizens.

2. Many data, such as those indicating travel times, are not collected regularly or systematically to permit comparisons of facets of a transportation system over time.

3. Citizen complaint information alone may give misleading signals. Reliance on this information is inadequate for program planning because it is not necessarily representative of community sentiment. People differ widely in their tendency to complain; some refrain because they do not know how to file complaints or because they believe their complaints would be ignored. Even to the extent complaint data could be useful, the information is seldom aggregated or systematically arrayed to indicate trends.

The effectiveness measures and data collection procedures in this report are intended to supplement — not replace — traditional traffic data or sophisticated transportation surveys and models. These are quite valuable. The additional recommended data are intended to correct the deficiencies just described, by providing information that reflects the impact of transportation systems on citizens. Such customer-oriented data should prove useful to those charged with local government transportation policies and programs.

III. Transportation Objectives and Suggested Effectiveness Measures

Setting Local Objectives

Intra-urban travel is rarely an end in itself. Rather, it facilitates satisfaction of other needs and objectives of individuals in the community. The general objective of local or community transportation services may be expressed as follows:

> *To provide access to desired destinations such as employment, shopping, and community services or facilities in a safe, quick, comfortable, and convenient manner for all population groups of the community without causing major harmful side effects.*

This overall objective can be divided into six components:[1]

1. <u>Accessibility and Convenience</u>: To provide residents of the community with reasonable access to an adequate choice of important destinations such as employment, personal services, and recreation.

2. <u>Time</u>: To minimize or at least keep within reasonable limits the travel time between home and such destinations as for employment, personal services, and community facilities; and between community, commercial and government centers.

3. <u>Comfort</u>: To make travel comfortable for the drivers and passengers.

---

1. This is only one possible list of transportation objectives. Examples of other formulations are discussed in References 15, 32, 35, 43, and 55.

At times, attempts to improve performance according to one measure may result in adverse changes by other measures. For example, an improvement which decreases the number of traffic injuries might result in increased travel times. Clearly, policy makers need to consider trade-offs among objectives when considering proposed changes, and then make use of the appropriate effectiveness measures.

Exhibit 2 illustrates how data for measures of effectiveness might be summarized each year to form one type of status report for policy officials and local government managers.[3] This summary highlights the comparisons between the quality of transportation service being received by different population segments and indicates changes over time. It presents measurement data for one clientele classification, namely neighborhood. Note that some of the measures (as in the case of Measure 4, "Congestion duration," which pertains to travel links) would not be classified by neighborhood.

Presenting an array of effectiveness data can highlight problem areas. For instance, by revealing a significant worsening of performance according to a particular measure from the previous year or a significant decline in performance for some neighborhoods relative to others, such a summary may indicate the need for greater government attention or reconsideration of existing policies.[4]

As stated earlier, there is no automatic formula for identify-

---

3. Reference 42 contains an example of the presentation of transportation effectiveness indices in budgeting.

4. Before remedial action is taken, of course, further analysis may be necessary to identify causes of the problem, to determine possible correctives, and to estimate the costs and effects of alternative solutions.

Exhibit 2. ILLUSTRATIVE SUMMARY OF ANNUAL DATA ON SELECTED MEASURES OF EFFECTIVENESS[a]

	Measures of Effectiveness	Neighborhood									Total	
		I	II	III	IV	V	VI	VII	VIII	IX	1971	1970
Accessibility & Convenience	1. Percent of residents not within 5 minutes of public transit service	27	32	38	7	23	78	18	45	19	26	29
	2. Citizen perception of convenience (percent satisfied)	64	68	53	88	72	23	78	59	83	73	68
Travel Time	3. Average time required to travel between key origins and destinations (minutes)											
	a) Public transit	15	17	23	8	14	33	19	21	14	17	19
	b) Automobile	12	15	18	4	7	22	14	17	11	11	12
	4. Congestion duration (minutes)					Not Applicable					80	72
Comfort	5. Road quality index (percent of streets rated unsatisfactory)	3	7	8	4	8	15	2	7	12	7	9
	6. Citizen perception of comfort (percent satisfied)	83	81	73	91	85	54	78	75	79	71	68
Environ Quality	10. Noise levels (decibels - peaks)	48	45	50	40	55	75	60	80	75	60	56
	Percent of households not owning an automobile[b]	31	23	15	53	11	5	28	3	34	20	22

a. See Chapters III and IV for a full list of the identified measures of effectiveness and discussion of the nature and data collection approaches for each of the measures.

b. This is not a measure of effectiveness. Instead these data are intended to provide perspective on the degree of dependence on public transportation in each area. This problem is discussed in Measure 1 and Chapter V.

ing which measure or measures of effectiveness should be emphasized in a locality at a given time. This is ultimately a matter of judgment. The measures and procedures in this report cannot replace that judgment and should not be considered in that light. However, they can provide decision makers with a better basis for arriving at their judgments. This may happen, in the first place, during the initial process when a local government makes the effort to spell out its own transportation objectives. Then, after choosing specific measures of effectiveness to match these objectives (as illustrated in Exhibit 1 and described in the next chapter), the subsequent findings will form an orderly basis for seeing local conditions through an improved perspective. Community and citizen needs that currently may be overlooked or under-estimated can then be given due consideration by officials before they assign priorities for further transportation develop-ments.

IV. Effectiveness Measures and Data Collection Procedures

The effectiveness measures listed in Exhibit 1 are presented in greater detail in this chapter, along with the procedures for collecting the necessary data.

A major concern is to provide data collection procedures that are practical for local governments, requiring as little additional manpower and expenditure of funds as possible. Thus, wherever possible, the suggested procedures utilize data currently available to most local governments, placing them in a context to reflect accomplishment of an objective.

Over emphasis on data precision can lead to unnecessary data collection costs. Precise numbers are not required. Estimates of plus or minus 10 percent or more generally will be adequate to identify problem areas and permit comparisons over time and among population subgroups.

For most measures, data should be collected and analyzed annually to assist in program and policy formulation. Measures affected by seasonal variation require more frequent data collection. When data are used for management "control" (such as to assist in allocating street maintenance resources from month to month), more frequent measurement will be necessary. To support special in-depth analyses from time to time, additional data collection efforts may be necessary.

Demand for transportation service differs greatly between the commuter rush hours and daytime, evening, and weekend periods. A transportation system which moves an employee quickly and comfortably to and from work may be neglecting nonworkers who rely on transportation service for shopping, recreation, and other forms of participation in community life. The discussion of individual measures therefore suggests that some data should be gathered for both peak and off-peak travel periods.

The effectiveness of transportation services to an individual varies greatly with the modes of travel available to him. A person with unlimited access to an automobile normally experiences much different convenience, comfort, travel time, and cost than does a person who must rely upon public transit. Because of this, data on most measures should be collected and displayed for each mode, emphasizing particularly the differences in service for automobile and mass public transit users as well as for the jurisdiction as a whole.[1]

Data for Measures 2, 6, and 12 are collected by citizen survey. These data can be classified according to respondents who do and do not own an automobile, and according to their stated mode usage or preference as described in Measure 12. Measures 7, 8, and 9 are based on statistics easily stated separately by mode. Data for Measures 1 and 3 are collected separately for each mode. Measures 4, 5, 10, and 11 do not pertain to users of one mode only, and thus data on these measures would not normally require separation.

It is also desirable to provide a perspective on the degree of dependency on public transportation of clientele groups, especially by neighborhoods. Determining the degree of dependency upon public transportation is a complex issue. However, much relevant information is contained in census data on the number of automobiles owned per household. These automobile ownership data should be analyzed along with the effectiveness

---

1. One way of displaying these data is illustrated in Exhibit 2 for Measure 3.

data for each geographical area, and for other clientele groups where possible. Analysis of data by degree of automobile ownership is further discussed in the section below on Measure 1, and in Chapter V.

Besides distinguishing the level of transportation service for persons without access to automobiles, other segments of the population such as low income and handicapped persons also warrant special attention. Chapter V identifies some pertinent clientele subgroups and discusses methods for collecting effectiveness data for them.

We have attempted here to identify only that data which, when collected on a regular (at least annual) basis, can help provide a reasonable perspective of the overall status of the local transportation system.

Measure 1. Percent of Residents Not Within "X" Minutes of Public Transit Service or More Than One Hour From Key Destinations

Discussion

Accessibility, as used in this report, refers to the ability of persons to reach important community destinations such as work, shopping or recreational opportunities from their place of residence with reasonable expenditures of time and effort. This measure aims to determine the extent to which residents lack access to certain important destinations either because they lack means of travel or because such a large amount of travel time is required that they are discouraged from initiating the trip.

For this measure, we single out those persons either without access to automobiles, or those who prefer not to use them. We assume here that those with regular access to an automobile usually have "reasonable" access to important destinations.[2]

We suggest two parts to this measurement:

1.   Persons without access to automobile transportation must rely on public modes to reach destinations beyond walking distance. For them the availability of transit service within a reasonable walking distance from their residence is a crucial determinant of their ability to reach important points. Thus, we suggest the use of the measure *percent (or number) of residents not within "X" minutes of public transit service* as the measure of accessibility. To the extent possible, data from this measure should be keyed to persons without access to automobiles or who do not want to use automobiles. The walking distance, "X," should probably be about 5 to 10 minutes.

2.   Nearness to a transit stop alone does not necessarily guarantee a resident's accessibility as defined above. The transit routes may not go near important destinations or may require a large amount of travel time (including transfers) to reach these destinations.[3]   A trip requiring a large amount of time, perhaps over one hour, may be deferred or foregone because of the time required, thus making some destinations effectively inaccessible. Therefore, *the percent (or number) of persons more than one hour travel time from key destinations* is also suggested as part

---

2. In this discussion we have deviated somewhat from the meaning of the term "accessibility" as it is most commonly used in transportation modeling work. Such work often describes accessibility using concepts of "friction factors" which may be derived from such factors as trip time or other trip costs. Such a complex concept as this would be difficult and expensive to translate into a form usable by local governments for the limited purposes intended here.

3. In Measure 3, travel time itself is discussed as a measure of transportation effectiveness.

of this measure.[4]

Infrequent transit may also discourage travel and thus limit accessibility. For this reason we suggest separate calculation of measurement data where service frequencies vary, as with peak and off-peak service. The influence of service frequency on discouraging travel is, however, measured more directly by Measure 3 (travel time).

Data Collection

The percent of residents not within "X" minutes of public transit service can be calculated by plotting transit stops on a base map showing population distribution for each neighborhood.[5] Around each transit stop the area is delineated from which the stop could be reached in a specified walking time, perhaps 5 to 10 minutes. In measuring distance to transit stops any physical barriers which might limit direct access to the transit stop should be considered. The number and percent of neighborhood residents living outside the designated walking distance would be considered as not having reasonable access to public transit.

Exhibit 3 illustrates this method. The circled areas around transit stops represent five minutes walking distance. Although one-quarter mile walking distance is often used as a service stand-

---

4. The effect of trip time on accessibility is discussed in greater detail by Reference 61. This report appears to confirm that it is reasonable to consider one hour as a reasonable limit beyond which most people, unless highly motivated, will avoid repeated travel. Designation of acceptable time may vary with the community.

5. Most cities have access to census information which is disaggregated by district or block. As census data ages, rough updatings of the population distribution would be needed.

Exhibit 3. ACCESSIBILITY OF PUBLIC TRANSIT: ILLUSTRATION OF MAPPING PROCEDURE.

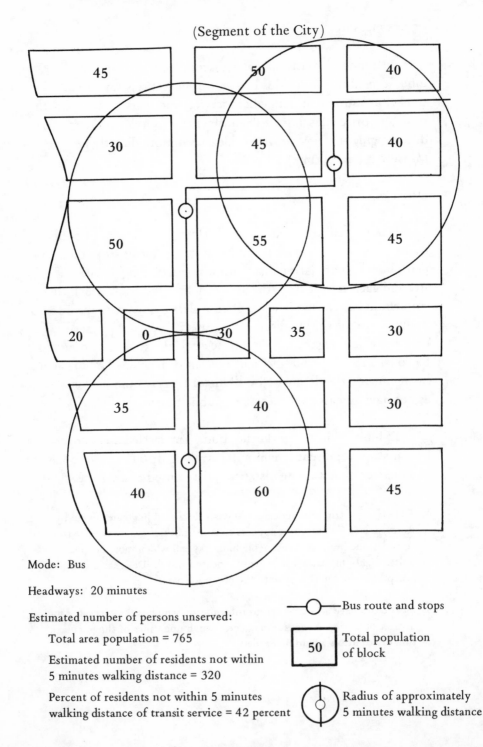

(Segment of the City)

Mode: Bus

Headways: 20 minutes

Estimated number of persons unserved:

    Total area population = 765

    Estimated number of residents not within
    5 minutes walking distance = 320

    Percent of residents not within 5 minutes
    walking distance of transit service = 42 percent

—O— Bus route and stops

50   Total population of block

Radius of approximately 5 minutes walking distance

ard for public transit stops for low density areas, the distance
that people are willing to walk depends on many factors such
as: trip purpose; time available; the age, vigor, income, and
preference of the individual; weather conditions, and the
physical attractiveness and crowdedness of the path. Jurisdictions attempting to quantify this measure may use one-quarter
mile as the acceptable distance, an actual walking time standard
such as five minutes, or another standard more suitable to local
conditions and preferences. The citizen survey proposed in
Measure 12 could be used to assist a community in establishing
a standard representing the distance local citizens are willing to
walk to reach transit service.

The mapping technique estimates the area and the number of residents without reasonable access to transit service.
However, it is likely that many of these residents own or have
regular access to an automobile and therefore may not require
or desire transit service. It is also desirable, then, to provide an
estimate of the number of residents who depend on transit
service and do not have reasonable access to it.

Persons most likely to rely on public transit (thereby
warranting special consideration in application of this measure)
are (a) members of families without automobiles, (b) adults
in families who do not have regular access to an automobile
(such as housewives without an automobile during daytime
hours), (c) adults who are unable or unwilling to drive, or (d)
children or adolescents unable to drive but able to use public
transit independently. An estimate of the number of persons
in each neighborhood in these categories can be made based
on automobile ownership and family size data from census
counts or citizen survey data. (See Measure 12.) This information would also help in estimating the proportion of neighborhood residents who rely on a public mode for travel.

22

In interpreting data for each neighborhood, it is also important to consider subgroups which have special need for transit service. On each map rest homes, convalescent hospitals and facilities for the care of handicapped persons could be identified.

Infrequent service may also limit accessibility. A three-minute walk to service available every hour is clearly not equivalent to a three-minute walk to service every ten minutes. Separate maps and estimates of the number of residents not having reasonable access to transit service could be prepared for each level of service frequency, where frequencies or "headways" vary substantially, as for peak and off-peak travel periods. Very infrequent service may in itself connote inaccessibility. However, because it is difficult to estimate the degree to which a specific service infrequency discourages travel (limits accessibility), citizen satisfaction with service frequency is directly assessed by Measure 2. (Note: Waiting times at transit stops are measured directly in Measure 3.)

Procedures for estimating the second part of this measure—percent of persons more than one hour from key destinations—are discussed under Measure 3. The population served by those travel links that exceed one hour would be utilized for this measure.

Measure 2. Citizen Perception of Travel Convenience

Discussion

In Chapter II convenience is defined as the effort required in traveling to desired destinations. To a considerable extent this is closely related to the notion of accessibility discussed in Measure 1, and to travel time which will be discussed in Measures 3 and 4.

In this measure we deal with convenience as perceived by the citizens themselves. It involves such factors as:

- Proximity of transit stops to home or destinations.

- Frequency of transit service during peak and off-peak hours.

- Number of transfers required to reach important destinations.

- Availability of information about transit routes and schedules.

- Availability of parking during peak and off-peak hours.

- Understandability of street identification, traffic signs and signals.

The last two factors apply primarily to automobile users. The others pertain to common carriers. The perceptions of transit users and non-users of the convenience of travel by public mode are of considerable importance to local governments.

Data Collection

Actual figures on the relative usage of the various modes, of course, express the "votes" of citizens on convenience. But these "votes" also simultaneously reflect people's response to other factors such as those discussed under Measures 1, 3, 6, and 9 and the availability of private automobiles. Thus, usage information alone does not indicate which of these factors are most influential.

Citizen perception information is probably best obtained

by direct citizen surveys. Attitude surveys of samples of citizens are becoming useful in addressing a variety of government problems and are increasing in use throughout the country.

For this measure, both on-board (transit) and at-home (by telephone or in person) surveys are possibilities. In many jurisdictions an at-home survey may require a large, uneconomical sample size to contact a sufficient number of transit users. Thus the on-board survey appears to be the most direct way of reaching public transit users. On the other hand, an at-home survey will provide feedback from persons not using public transit on their perceptions of transit service convenience.

The type of questions on convenience that could be included in such surveys is illustrated in the Appendix.[6] Survey procedures and problems are discussed further under Measure 12. Note that the function of this measure is to obtain information on how citizens *perceive* convenience. Regardless of actual frequency, proximity, and availability of transportation services (which are considered in other measures), information on citizen perceptions should be an important concern of officials. (The type of government action that may be appropriate will depend on the relationship between perception information and data from other related measures.)

Data on this measure would be expressed as *the percent of respondents who replied in specific ways to survey questions,* e.g., the percent of respondents who stated that the frequency of public transit was "not nearly frequent enough" (Questions 14 c and d of Appendix). Such data should be classified by respondents identified as transit users versus nonusers, as well as for all respondents in the total sample. Data should also be separated by

6. Particularly, Questions 14 a-f, 15 a-e, 17, and 18.

automobile ownership or availability of an automobile for personal use.

The information from the survey questions can also provide clues as to corrective action that may appear needed.

Measure 3. Time Required To Travel Between Major Origin and Destination Points

Discussion

The length of time required to travel between two points is certainly one of the most important tests of a transportation system's effectiveness.

Presently some local governments and most regional transportation planning bodies use "speed and delay runs" to obtain data on travel times along major traffic arteries. These studies show the speed profile of an arterial and help to identify reasons for changes in traffic speed. These data are used to enhance the quality of traffic flow by signalization, establishment of reasonable speed, and other engineering improvements. Such data and the procedures used can be of considerable help for this measure. The census also obtains a limited amount of travel time data, but these are collected infrequently so care must be taken to avoid using outdated information.

These special studies, however, usually do not furnish data which can be used to compare travel times along links[7] in

---

7. "Link" in this context applies to the most direct route connecting terminals of typical trips listed below.

the transportation network for different points in time or for different modes serving the same link.

The measure suggested here indicates the effectiveness of the transportation system by collecting data on time required to reach major employment, shopping, and recreational opportunities from areas of high residential density and to travel between selected downtown points. Travel time along these links should be estimated for both autos and public transit.

For this measure we have not focused on average travel time per person or per family because this is partly a function of various activities within an urban area. The main function of this measure is to permit comparisons by mode and over time (i.e., from year to year), rather than to compare, for example, the work travel time of different neighborhoods.

In many cities, downtown pedestrian congestion is a growing problem. In such jurisdictions, walking times between downtown points might also be sampled. The problem of pedestrian congestion is suggested for consideration by each jurisdiction, although it is not discussed here in detail.

Data Collection

Clearly it would be impractical to collect travel time data for all possible trips in an urban area. Instead, travel time measurements suggested here are quite selective, representing a simplified approach. We feel that for the limited purpose of presenting comparative data on travel times within the jurisdiction, it is better to be selective and thereby avoid excessive data collection costs. For this measure, a few focal points of urban travel are selected which represent important community destinations such as those trips listed below. The time required to travel between these terminals would be used as this measure.

Travel Time Measurement Routes

Trip Purpose	Typical Terminals	Travel Time Usually Undertaken	Type of Route
A. Work trip	Residential area and employment centers	Peak	Arterials
B. Shopping in central business districts	Residential areas and the central business district	Off-peak	Arterials
C. Shopping in regional shopping centers and local shopping areas	Residential areas and nearby local shopping centers	Off-peak	Connectors
D. Recreation	Residential areas and a nearby large recreation site	Off-peak	Connectors
E. Business-cross town	Various points within the central business district	Off-peak	Connectors

Selection of the important focuses of travel for the area is the crucial step in this measure. For trips A through D, one terminal would be areas of high residential density, usually one per service area or neighborhood (delineated as suggested in Chapter V). Selection of the employment, commercial, and recreation focuses of urban travel relevant to each neighborhood is somewhat more difficult.

Most communities will be able to identify important urban travel focuses by use of local use maps, traffic volume data, and knowledge of the location of frequently used community centers.

Most metropolitan areas have origin-destination surveys[8] or metropolitan transportation models available which can be very helpful in identifying frequently traveled links in the transportation network. Selection of destination points can be based in part on these data.

Besides identifying links presently traveled with high frequency, other links should be included which, though not presently traveled with high frequency, are nevertheless "socially desirable." An example of this would be a link from a low income neighborhood with a high unemployment rate to employment centers which could potentially use the type of labor available in the neighborhood. Careful selection of destination points can help to identify neighborhoods isolated from community interaction by poor transportation service. The major reason for not relying solely upon origin-destination surveys for identification of all key links is that data from such surveys represent trips currently undertaken with high frequency. They may fail to identify trips foregone due to lack of adequate transportation service or links felt in need of development.

Besides travel between residential neighborhoods and important community destinations, it may also be desirable to include links connecting nonresidential points (E). Vitality of the business district is often influenced by mobility within the downtown area. To test this, travel links should also be designated between downtown points and between other nonresidential points important to the community.

We estimate that perhaps a total of 15 to 30 links might be

---

8. Cost and methodology of origin-destination surveys is summarized in Reference 24. See also Reference 18 for discussion of one application of O-D information in trip distribution modeling.

sufficient for most communities. Exhibit 4 illustrates these travel links.

The selected links probably should not extend beyond the borders of the jurisdiction undertaking the measurements— since the jurisdiction will have little, or no, control over external travel routes.[9]

Since travel is very much dependent upon the dynamics of urban growth, some links may be added or deleted over time so that travel links used in measurements remain generally representative of trips frequently undertaken. However, we emphasize that to identify changes in residential travel times, it is important to collect comparable data from a fairly stable list of links for a series of years.

After representative links have been selected, travel time by each available mode is measured along each link. To obtain automobile travel times, actual driving time between the two points could be measured by government personnel. Public transportation travel times could either be calculated from schedules published by transit agencies or by direct measurement. Direct measurement of public transit would involve boarding the vehicle at a stop near the center of the neighborhood. Travel time would be measured from the first stop to the stop nearest the typical destinations chosen. Factors for initial waiting time (such as one-half the headway), time spent at transfer points, and walking time to destination should also be indicated.

Time measurements for automobiles begin with the start

---

9. These links, however, may be part of areawide travel routes, and good community transportation planning requires coordination with metropolitan transportation planning.

30

Exhibit 4: TRAVEL LINKS BETWEEN MAJOR ORIGIN
AND DESTINATION POINTS

City Limits

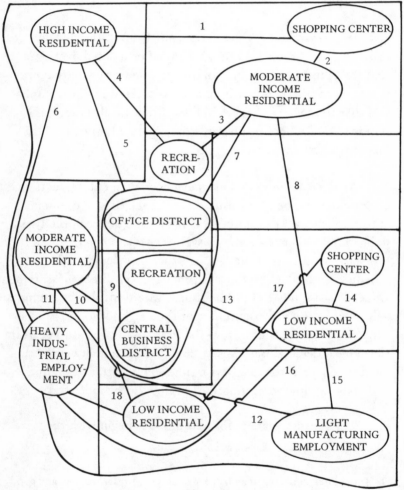

City Limits

of a trip at a point central to a residential neighborhood and end at a point central to the pertinent destination area. In each case, the least-mileage route should be selected for measurement. Procedures for data collection should be standardized so that data collected by different personnel and in different years are comparable. The specific starting and ending points and routes should be noted so annual data on each link may be compared.

Measurement data for both automobiles and public transit should be gathered on each link during at least two periods in a year to reflect seasonal fluctuations of traffic volume. Tests should be scheduled to avoid holidays unless, of course, there is special community interest in travel problems at these times. Measurements on each route would be conducted daily for at least three consecutive weekdays at approximately the same times of day. Travel times gathered on the consecutive days would be averaged to produce the travel time for the trip section. (The ranges and distributions of trip times could also be examined to provide additional insights.)

Measurement data should be gathered in such a way that they are also comparable between modes. Such factors as the time required to find parking for automobiles, waiting time at transit stops, and walking time do complicate comparisons of travel time data among modes. Our current suggestions here are to make estimates of typical times for these individual arrangements. For example, automobile travel-to-work time could include an estimate of typical time for walking from parking to work. For transit, travel-to-work time could include an estimate for walking to stops, waiting for transit vehicle, and walking from final stop to work location. These estimates have the disadvantage of averaging out wide variations in actual time in transit. However, for this measure, *precise* total trip times are not needed.

Data obtained are not intended to be representative of exact travel times experienced by individual residents on regular trips to the destinations. Each residential origin point represents a multiblock area and there are likely to be many specific routes which a traveler may select. Instead, time data should be useful in annual comparisons of the same route and as general comparisons between different routes.

The travel time estimates (by mode) from the 15 to 30 links could be arranged or combined in a variety of ways. For instance, they can be weighted by: (1) the expected relative volumes of travel on the links; (2) the average length of each trip; or (3) the average speed of travel along each link. It is cautioned, however, that should such weighting be used, especially by travel volume, the data may no longer reflect the social importance of selected links.

For trips originating in residential areas, it is desirable to consider the relative use and dependency of residents of each neighborhood on public and private modes. For example, high transit travel times may be of minor concern in a neighborhood where almost everyone has access to, and uses, an automobile.

As suggested earlier, automobile ownership information can provide a rough indication of automobile availability and can be obtained from census and citizen survey data. These estimates will be helpful in analyzing the importance of time data for each mode from each neighborhood.

Measure 4. Congestion — Duration and Severity of Delay

Discussion

A special concern is the magnitude of major traffic congestion in the community. This measure is designed to indicate both the duration and severity of congestion at peak travel periods. It is distinct from Measure 3 because it focuses directly upon the major points of traffic or passenger congestion, rather than travel time over an entire link or over the entire city.

The use of both dimensions — duration and severity — of traffic congestion reflects a trade-off often implicit in planning for peak commuting periods. For example, a local jurisdiction may be able to decrease the delay which an individual traveler experiences due to traffic congestion by encouraging staggered work hours. But this may, at the same time, lengthen the time during which urban travel is disrupted due to peak hour congestion. On the other hand a jurisdiction may wish to limit intra-urban disruption of travel to a shorter period at the cost of decreasing the average speed of travel during the peak period.

Note that the problem here is not to determine or prove that there is congestion present (a condition that is usually readily observable). Rather it is to measure the degree of congestion and to estimate with reasonable certainty whether it is improving or worsening over time and by approximately how much.

It is necessary that the jurisdiction make some specific definition of what constitutes "congestion." Our suggestion is to define it as the time during which travel time between two points is at least some percentage (e.g., 25 percent) greater than travel time at some standard travel speed (e.g., 30 mph) between the same two points during off-peak hours. The "duration" can be defined as the length of time during which travel time exceeds this "standard" percentage. Congestion "severity" can be defined as the maximum ratio of travel time to the "standard" during the observation period. [10]

---

10. Some thought might also be given to a measure that reflects the number of people involved, e.g., "the number of people-minutes of congestion."

Data Collection

The duration and severity of congestion would be measured for each heavily traveled artery which connects intensely developed business or industrial sections with residential areas. Travel time between two points along such routes would be measured at intervals during peak periods and compared with nonpeak periods. The duration of congestion for each artery would be the number of minutes from the beginning to the end of the period of severe traffic congestion. One possible way to gather necessary data, of course, is to make a series of runs in vehicles and time these runs. Another method which would require less manpower is suggested here.[11]

Except where a special express bus lane is provided or where there are numerous pick-up points in the congested area, buses are slowed by traffic congestion to approximately the same degree as other vehicular traffic using roadways. Two points along the bus route in the jurisdiction, perhaps one downtown and the other near the end of the artery congestion, would be designated as measurement points.

Prior to the peak time period, time checks would begin. A "clocker" would be placed at each of the check points to record the time of arrival of each bus, and its license plate or serial number. The watches of the two inspectors would be synchronized. Observations would be taken continuously during the commuting period. This would measure the time

---

11. The duration of congestion is usually measured by use of "load factors." This is a concept which may be considered as an alternative (see Reference 23 for a discussion of load factors). However, we suggest another method for general use because it more clearly demonstrates the effect of congestion upon users of arterial routes.

required for the buses to travel between these two points during the congestion period. These travel times could be stated as percentages of some "standard" such as the time it would take to travel between the check points at, say, an average of thirty miles per hour.

Exhibit 5 illustrates data on congestion duration and severity that might result . Using the given definitions of congestion duration and severity, the hypothetical travel link has a congestion duration of 80 minutes and a severity of 202 percent of the "standard."

The greater the frequency of rush hour bus service, the larger the number of observations which can be obtained. Time samples should be collected for the same road section on a series of subsequent weekdays and averaged to determine the duration of congestion on each arterial. Data should be collected seasonally. Days for each seasonal set of observations should be selected to separate good from poor weather conditions.

The use of public transit vehicles to measure arterial congestion is only one possibility for gathering these data. It appears to offer two advantages. Vehicles normally travel along the arterials where congestion occurs and the vehicles' routes are known, permitting the placement of clockers at key points on the routes to time individual vehicles. The disadvantages are that on some major routes there may not be bus routes or the bus vehicles may stop too often or too long to produce measurements that seem appropriate to represent automobile congestion. Other methods of data collection certainly can be devised using traffic counts and speed measurements. A count of the number of cars per hour passing a point, for example, may be useful as a

Exhibit 5. EXAMPLE OF TRAFFIC CONGESTION DATA

Time Required to Travel Between Points at "Standard" of 30 MPH Average Speed[a]	Time of Measurement (Origin)	Measured Travel Time (Minutes)	Measured Travel Time as a Percent of the "Standard"[b]	
	7:00 a.m.	6.58 minutes	109%	
	7:10	7.35	122	
	7:20	7.63	127	⌐
	7:30	8.94	149	
	7:40	10.52	175	
	7:50	11.02	183	Duration
6.0 minutes	8:00	12.15	202 [c]	of
	8:10	10.43	173	Congestion
	8:20	9.20	153	
	8:30	8.34	139	
	8:40	7.56	126	└
	8:50	7.41	124	
	9:00	7.38	123	

a. Distance between check points in these hypothetical observations is three miles.

b. The duration of the congestion time in this example is from approximately 7:20 a.m. - 8:40 a.m. or 80 minutes. This is based on defining "congestion" as an increase in travel time between the check points of 25 percent above the time traveled at 30 miles per hour.

c. Severity of delay is defined as the maximum percentage—which here is 202 percent.

measure of congestion. However, this has the drawback that traffic count data simultaneously reflect both the amount and speed of traffic. Thus, the measure of traffic volume passing a point may be equally low during congested and noncongested periods.

Where a travel route serves only automobiles, congestion periods can be estimated using measurement of travel speed past a designated point. The travel speed during peak periods can be measured by radar or stop watches.

Measure 5. Index of Road Surface Quality ("Bumpiness")

Discussion

The comfort, and often the safety, of automobile passengers depends to a large extent upon the quality of the street pavement.

Presently, local governments determine road maintenance schedules by the number of citizen complaints received, age of the street, and field observations.

Complaint data are a useful but insufficient basis for allocating street maintenance efforts. Residents of some neighborhoods may have become accustomed to deficiencies and no longer register complaints. Other residents may not know how to file a complaint or believe that complaining is futile. On the other hand, because a community often has some chronic complainers, government officials may disregard urgent requests for service because these are not distinguished from the large number of trivial complaints received.

Pavements do not deteriorate at a uniform rate. Type

of soil or road base, moisture, type and volume of traffic, original quality of construction, and climate are among the factors which influence the durability of the pavement. Age of the pavement and maintenance records may, therefore, be a misleading indicator of the need for maintenance service.

Public works inspectors also conduct occasional observations of street condition. Such inspections, though, are usually not systematic and are concentrated on primary roadways. This limits the usefulness of inspection data for comparing road conditions between neighborhoods or among arterial and residential streets.

In some locales, police personnel are requested to report pavement deficiencies during their regular patrols. Because this task is not of prime importance relative to law enforcement duties, resulting data may be quite unreliable, varying greatly with the time available and the interest of each officer. In any case, the data are seldom retained and tabulated so as to be useful for evaluation.

Data Collection

Ratings of pavement quality should be made using a procedure and a sufficiently precise measurement scale so that observations of street condition made by different personnel and at different times and locations can be compared.

Various mechanical devices have been constructed to measure the surface quality of roads objectively. Available instruments such as the Bureau of Public Roads "roughometer" and the Portland Cement Company "roadmeter" vary in complexity and sensitivity, but basically are intended to record the road's bumpiness. [12]

In April 1972, we tested the roughometer to assess and compare the conditions of local roads of various neighborhoods of a county. [13] The device measures "inches of roughness per mile." However, its limited availability currently throughout the country probably makes this method impractical for regular monitoring of road quality by many local governments. [14]

A simpler mechanism capable of distinguishing between three or four degrees of road roughness probably could be developed inexpensively.[15] The instrument need only be able to record roughly the severity and frequency of surface deficiencies.

The rating of surface quality could be expressed as a value on a scale from one to four, calibrated to the degree of comfort likely to be experienced by an automobile passenger.

---

12. For evaluation of some existing measurement devices, see References 34, 52, 55, 59, and 60.

13. This test was funded and conducted separately from the development of components of this report (see Reference 6 for results).

14. Direct cost of operation of the roughometer was approximately $200 per day (including labor and equipment rental).

15. For example, it might be possible to improvise a mechanism using a pendulum, a bell, or some other type of device capable of roughly indicating the degree of road roughness.

The inspection procedure should be standardized for any factor that might influence the data, independent of road surface quality. For instance, the speed, travel path of the measurement device, the vehicle's suspension system, and weather conditions should be similar in the tests.

Continuous monitoring of the condition of all streets within a jurisdiction is too costly for most communities. However, inspection of a sample of streets, carefully selected to be representative of all streets, can provide a basis for allocating road maintenance resources.

The sample of streets should be selected for inspection from census tracts, service areas, or other homogeneous subunits of the jurisdiction. So that the sample is indeed representative of road conditions throughout the neighborhood, a statistically sound procedure must be used to select inspection locations. Inspectors should not be allowed to choose the measurement locations because, consciously or subconsciously, they are likely to exert a bias.

The number of observations made in each neighborhood would depend upon inspection resources available and the degree of accuracy desired.

Measure 6. Citizen Perception of Travel Comfort

Discussion

Besides being a concern in itself, the comfort of public transit vehicles relative to automobiles is one of the factors affecting choice of mode as well as the frequency of travel. Some factors relevant to transit passenger comfort are:

• Crowdedness of vehicle (and privacy)

- Noise level within vehicle

- Temperature and odors within vehicle

- Jerkiness of the ride (including the frequency of stops and starts)

- Forced exposure to inclement weather

- Internal cleanliness of vehicles

Data Collection

For public transit, comfort factors such as those listed above can probably best be tested in an on-board survey of passengers or by an at-home survey conducted in person or by telephone. Illustrative questions of the type that might be included in a survey on comfort characteristics are shown in the Appendix, particularly Questions 13 a-f, and 15 f and g.

As noted in the discussion of Measure 2, an on-board survey has the advantage of being an effective way of reaching public transit users. An at-home survey in many jurisdictions might require a large, uneconomical sample size to reach a sufficient number of transit users. On the other hand, the citizen survey can obtain feedback on perception of transit vehicle comfort by non-users of public transit. Comparisons of the responses of users and non-users may provide an indication of the extent to which comfort factors may limit the use of transit. Both surveys might be undertaken each year to permit comparison of the comfort of available modes. Survey procedures and problems are discussed further under Measure 12.

For automobile users, many of the factors listed above,

such as vehicle cleanliness and air-conditioning, are under their personal — not governmental — control. Therefore, questions on the quality of personally owned vehicles are probably unnecessary in the citizen survey. However, we do suggest that a question on the subject of road quality or "bumpiness" be included for automobile users (such as Question 19 in the Appendix). The information obtained from this would be considered along with the direct field measurement for Measure 5 (surface quality).

This measure would be expressed as the percent of respondents who replied in specific ways to the survey questions, e.g., the percent of respondents who felt that the public transit vehicles are either "fairly" or "very" noisy (Question 13 of the Appendix).

Data should be provided for respondents identified in the survey as transit users, non-users, and for the group of respondents as a whole. Data may further be separated by automobile ownership or availability of an automobile for personal use.

Measure 7. Rate of Transportation-Related Accidents: Injuries, Deaths, and Property Damage

Discussion

Property damage and physical injury to users and non-users of the transportation system is an important community concern. Traffic and police departments collect data on accidents involving vehicles and pedestrians. These data are used to monitor trends and identify correctable hazards.

To measure the consequences of transportation policies and programs fully, transportation-related injuries, deaths and incidents of property damage must be recorded for all modes. The safety of each mode may be compared on the basis of number of incidents by type.

Data Collection

Local police agencies record automobile traffic accident data in great detail. Such records may slightly underestimate the number of some types of incidents, especially those involving pedestrian injuries, due to incidents not reported. If nonreporting is suspected to be common, data may be partially validated by citizen survey. Injuries in public transportation vehicles or facilities are recorded by operating companies for insurance purposes.

Accident data often inhibit comparisons of safety in different neighborhoods and transportation modes. Data are recorded by victims' addresses rather than by place of accident. Local agencies define incidents differently. Levels of recorded detail vary. Minor alterations of accident report forms and procedures could overcome these difficulties.

To make annual comparisons, accident data should take account of changes in the use of each mode. Such modification is especially necessary in areas experiencing rapid changes in population, economic activity, or shifts on land use patterns. For instance, statistics that otherwise might be quite puzzling could be clarified by a notation about the opening of a new shopping center.

Transportation-related accidents, injuries, deaths, and property damage should preferably be stated and compared for each mode as the number per vehicle-mile (or per 100 million miles) traveled, or as numbers of occurrences modified by a percentage of a base year.

A number of methods are available for estimating percent annual travel volume for an area. Three possible ways to standardize data are:

1. Vehicles are counted regularly on major arterials in most jurisdictions. Annual traffic volumes can be compared either by using a standard formula to translate vehicle counts into vehicle miles or by stating annual data as a percent change from a base year.

2. In some jurisdictions motor vehicle fuel sales are recorded for tax purposes. The number of vehicle miles traveled may be obtained by multiplying the gallons of motor vehicle fuel sold by a factor representing an estimate of miles traveled per gallon of fuel (under typical driving conditions for the locality).

3. In some metropolitan areas vehicle registration statistics may also provide a useful basis for estimating changes in volume of urban travel.

Public transit operating agencies usually estimate traffic volume, expressed either in passenger volumes or vehicle miles traveled, or both.

Measure 8. Number of Crime Incidents Related to Transportation

Discussion

Crime incidents on transportation facilities and aboard public transit vehicles affect public mobility. Public apprehension about personal safety while using common carriers or transit facilities may limit the frequency of travel, choice of mode, and travel to certain areas.

Total number of reported robberies and physical attacks at bus stops and transit stations or in transit should be listed for the urban area and by neighborhood. The number of robberies of bus and taxi drivers and total dollar loss due to vandalism of public vehicles is also significant.

Transit crime concentrated in an area will lessen travel and the use of public modes by residents or visitors of the neighborhood. Thus, data on crime incidents at transit stops is much more meaningful if it is disaggregated by neighborhood.

Where a high number of incidents occur in a neighborhood, detailed analysis of the specific location, type of offense, time of day, and victim characteristics may serve as the basis for designing preventive action.

Data Collection

Data on criminal incidents can be obtained from police reports. Where transportation crime statistics are not recorded separately, slight revision of police report forms might be advisable to make data more easily accessible. Some transit agencies collect crime data and, in most cases, estimate the cost of vandalism damage annually.

Data for this measure should also be adjusted to reflect changes in population, expressed as a crime rate for the jurisdiction (e.g., crimes per 10,000 population), to make comparisons over time meaningful.

Measure 9. Cost Per Trip

Discussion

Citizens are, of course, vitally concerned with how much their trips cost them. In addition, choice of mode and frequency of travel can be affected by trip costs. At least five types of cost can be identified:

1.   Dollar outlays (fares, tolls, fuel, parking fees) directly related to length and frequency of trips.

2.   Variable dollar costs borne directly by the user, but less directly related to individual trips (e.g., vehicle maintenance costs).

3.   Long-term dollar costs borne directly by the user but not varying greatly with amount of travel (e.g., insurance, vehicle amortization).

4.   Hidden costs (to users or non-users) implicit in the trip but not normally apparent as a consequency of the trip (e.g., road maintenance, transit subsidies, new facility construction, community pollution control costs). This type of cost frequently will be reflected eventually in taxes, although sometimes (as when air pollution causes paint damage) private costs are generated.

5.   Nonmonetary costs to the user resulting directly from the trip (e.g., fatigue, stress, opportunity cost of time, and air pollution effect on health).

This measure concentrates on dollar costs of travel, particularly those most readily apparent to the individual citizen. The major nonmonetary personal costs to the user are assessed directly by other measures identified elsewhere in this report. The difficulty with placing a dollar value on such factors as travel time and the questionable meaningfulness of monetarizing non-pecuniary effects have influenced our preference for considering monetary and nonmonetary costs separately.

For this measure we suggest the inclusion only of dollar out-lays directly related to the length and frequency of trips (the first type of cost cited above). Although this choice is somewhat arbitrary, it has the advantage of reflecting those costs that are of most immediate concern to users.

Data Collection

Much research has been conducted to quantify better the cost per mile of travel by each mode. For instance, cost per mile of travel by automobile varies due to differences in the initial vehicle cost, average operating costs, automobile risk, topography of the area, traffic speed and flow, and many other factors.

Using the links connecting each residential area to major community destinations identifed in Measure 3, the cost of these important trips should be displayed for each mode.

Figures on transit fares and tolls are readily available for each link examined. Parking charges may vary somewhat at the destination — sometimes greatly within an area of a few blocks. However, for these purposes, some typical figure for parking cost can be readily obtained. Automobile fuel costs present the major difficulty. They vary somewhat with travel speed, fre-quency of starts and stops, and size of car. Considerable research on fuel costs has provided estimates of per mile costs modified by such factors as speed and grade. [16]

Measure 10. Noise Levels Along Transportation Corridors and Number of Persons Possibly Affected

Discussion

Noise produced by automobile, rail and other modes of transportation, and machines used in the construction or repair of streets harm the overall living environment for pedestrians, workers, and residents near transportation corridors. Research has been conducted on human perception and response to transportation-related noise. [17] The chart below, for example, shows the effect of various levels of traffic noise on conversation.

Effect of Noise Level on Conversation[18]

Outdoor Traffic Noise Level dbA (decibels on A scale)	For Satisfactory Speech Communication Outdoors, Raised Voice Is Needed at:
55	10 to 40 feet
65	5 to 10 feet
75	1 to 2 feet

One prominent study measured noise levels at curbside on

16. For example, see Reference 25.

17. See References 16, 41, 47, and 49.

18. Reference 16.

some major arterials in London that reached peaks of 90 decibels.

Noise from transportation varies with the type and condition of vehicles, road surface, road grade (especially heavy vehicles) and the use of horns and bells. Other factors affecting the noise level experienced by nonpassengers are distance of individuals from the roadway, amount of noise screening, volume and speed of traffic flow, vehicle acceleration and deceleration, and weather conditions.

This measure is expressed as the level of noise at a standard distance from major arterials. Whenever possible the measure should also indicate the number of citizens who are subjected to potentially harmful noise levels.

Data Collection

Noise level experienced by "nonpassengers" can be monitored by two complementary methods — direct measurement and citizen survey.

Direct measurements may be taken with a portable sound level meter. An instrument which measures noise levels only is inexpensive and easy to operate. Many local governments currently use such devices regularly.[19] Data may be based on estimate of average traffic noise or on maximum noise level.

It is recommended that noise level be measured periodically, perhaps quarterly, at specific locations where noise produced by transportation may be bothersome to groups of people.

19. For discussion of noise level measurement devices, see References 41, 49, 57, and 63.

A major criteria for the selection of these measurement points would be the way sites adjacent to noisy traffic are being used. Residential concentrations, outdoor recreational sites, office firms, and apartment and hotel complexes located along major highways or rail lines may experience some degree of disturbance from vehicular noise. Particular emphasis should be given to measuring the transportation noise near hospitals and other facilities where actual harm or suffering may be caused by high noise levels. Zoning and land use maps may help identify locations to be measured.

Sites for measurement of noise level should be added in response to changes in traffic patterns and deleted where several measurements over a period of time show that noise is not a serious problem. Special sound level measurement may also be desirable at transportation construction sites where heavy machinery is in use.

The exact location of the device at a measurement site should be specifically stated in procedures so that readings made at different times and by different personnel can be compared. The location should be carefully chosen so that measurement data are not affected significantly by non-transportation-related sounds, or by traffic sounds reflected by large signs, buildings or nearby topographical features. Most devices are designed to be placed about four feet from the ground and 25 to 100 feet from the center of the nearest traffic lane during measurements, depending on the type of traffic. Measurement procedure details should be standardized for tests made for a jurisdiction. Bibliographic references at the end of this report and sound meter instructions will assist local governments in drafting measurement procedures.

Most sound level data are stated in decibels measured

on the "A" scale (dbA) to show sound pitch. The "A" scale for decibel measurement is weighted to emphasize higher sound frequencies because these are more annoying to the human ear.[20] To record the peak sound level, the duration of tests may be very brief at each site. Separate data should be collected at morning and evening peak hours of travel and the off-peak traffic period (9:30 a.m. to 4 p.m.). Weather conditions may influence readings, so data should not be collected during high winds or when the pavement is wet.

Data for this measure might initially be stated as an average maximum-sound level at a specific distance from a roadway. To indicate the community impact of noise produced by transportation sources, it is probably more meaningful to state data in terms of number of persons affected by noise of a certain level. Estimates of geographical population distribution can probably be obtained from the community's planning agency or directly from census data. Since high noise levels may occur at work locations, it may be desirable to obtain rough estimates of the affected population in commercial areas.

Equal-noise-level contour maps have been used to illustrate the noise levels at various distances from a transportation route. Such a map overlaid on a land use or population density map may may be especially useful when relating sound levels to the land use and number of people affected.

A question may be included in the citizen survey (see Appendix, Question 13c) to measure the perception of disturbance due to transportation-related noise. Citizen surveys appear to be an unreliable method of measuring absolute noise levels

---

20. Reference 17 discusses human perception of noise and its measurement.

experienced by residents.[21]   However, surveys do appear to be
useful in identifying areas with intermittently loud noises (due
to such causes as rapid acceleration) or areas which have experienced a recent sharp increase in the noise level. Survey data can
thus help identify locations where further sound level measurement is advisable.

Measure 11. Air Pollution Attributable To Transportation Sources and Number of Persons Possibly Affected

Discussion

Emissions from internal combustion engines in automobiles
and some other transportation modes can be a serious health
hazard to inhabitants of urbanized areas. Transportation vehicles
are the chief source of carbon monoxide, lead and hydrocarbon
air pollution, and about one-half of nitrogen oxide pollution in
metropolitan areas, nationwide.

The health danger to humans from these pollutants is
demonstrated by laboratory tests. In one test on humans
an eight-hour exposure to carbon monoxide in a concentration
of 10 to 15 parts per million (PPM) caused the loss of some
brain functions. If repeated over a period of time, such exposure could contribute to lung disease. Concentrations of 50
to 100 PPM caused more serious injury to heart and lungs,
dizziness and the loss of some mental and physical abilities.
Smaller concentrations than these also appreciably contribute
to physical problems and thus will be of concern to most
jurisdictions.

---

21. See Reference 5.

Regular commuters and pedestrians are exposed to such high levels for brief periods. In a measurement on one traffic corridor in Washington, D. C., the carbon monoxide level reached a concentration of 93 PPM. Persons who reside or work along commuter routes will be affected over time by regular concentrations of transportation related pollutants. (See Reference 37.)

Data Collection

Measurement of transportation emissions is difficult because many industrial sources also emit pollutants into the atmosphere. Through careful analysis of air samples it is possible to identify the proportion of pollutants from transportation sources (particularly carbon monoxide and nitrogen oxide). Climatological factors such as wind circulation, temperature, and sunlight also vary the seriousness of hazard which inhabitants of an area experience and the relative severity of pollution in various parts of the urban area.

Governmental agencies regularly monitor overall air quality, the relative amounts of component pollutants, and the geographical distribution of air pollution within metropolitan areas. These data can be analyzed to obtain an average areawide level of transportation-related pollutants.

Transportation-related pollutants can also be measured directly by systematically gathering air samples along heavily traveled arterials. By analyzing these samples, it is possible to identify areas with serious concentrations of pollutants, and quantify the effect of transportation policies designed to alleviate pollution.

Data on transportation-related air pollutants are most readily available, stated as "parts per million." This is a sufficient, but minimal, statement of the system's effect on environmental quality. Data presented in this form fail to reflect directly the impact of pollution on the community. A more meaningful statement of the system's effect would be the "number of persons subjected to transportation pollution above a certain concentration." This could be obtained by displaying equal-pollutant-level contours on a residential density map. The number of travelers passing through the traffic corridor daily would also be included in the number of persons affected. The concentration levels could be selected according to information on "threshold" levels beyond which pollution begins to be aesthetically disturbing or a health hazard.

Data can also be obtained by collection of air samples along heavily traveled routes. When new arterials are opened or when traffic flow patterns shift substantially it is advisable that new measurement locations should be specified. Data should be collected at each measurement point at least seasonally, and displayed for policy purposes by geographical sub-area or averaged to indicate the areawide level of pollution from transportation sources.[22]

Where a single omission source such as an electrical power plant for a rail system exists, its emissions also should be measured.

Measure 12. Citizen Perception of Overall Adequacy of Transportation Services

Discussion

We have already suggested that direct feedback from

---

22. Reference 56 discusses a means of measuring emissions using traffic data.

citizens be obtained to measure various aspects of transportation, including convenience (Measure 2), comfort (Measure 6), and noise pollution (Measure 10). In Measure 12, we seek feedback on citizens' *overall* perception of the quality of transportation services.

As indicated earlier, citizen surveys can provide considerable specific information on transportation quality. They can provide important clues on the reasons for the lack of use of, or reasons for dissatisfaction with, certain transportation modes and may suggest possible ways to improve service.

Information should be obtained from users of the major modes of local transportation. Nonusers of any major mode should also be surveyed. It is important that public officials consider the degree to which nonuse of a particular mode indicates inadequacies in local transportation programs or policies. Responses from surveys may provide useful clues to necessary corrective actions.

Surveys are not the only way to get insights into citizen perceptions. Citizens also, of course, reflect their preferences by their actual use of available modes. Thus, figures on the ratio of transit passenger-trips to automobile passenger-trips may indicate important quality characteristics of the two types of travel mode. This ratio is not presented as a measure of effectiveness, however, because interpretation of the ratio relative to basic transportation system objectives presents serious difficulties. Depending on the local circumstances and characteristics of the existing local transportation system, it may appear desirable to increase or decrease this ratio. Low (or high) ratios relate to the complex set of local factors, and are not inherently bad or good.

Data Collection

As indicated under Measures 2 and 6, citizen surveys are probably the best way to obtain information on citizen perceptions. To keep costs down while making certain that data are reasonably representative of the entire community, proper sampling procedures should be used. Both a public transit on-board survey to assure that a large enough sample of transit users is obtained and an at-home survey are recommended. As with the other data collection procedures, these should be undertaken annually to provide trend data and indicate changes.

Surveys for various transportation purposes, particularly studies of travel behavior prior to new construction or major improvements of transportation routes, are fairly common. They often are considerably more detailed and extensive than what is necessary for the purposes here.

It is beyond the scope of this report to discuss citizen survey procedures in depth. References 58 and 60 provide some general guidance on survey techniques useful to local governments. Numerous other texts are available on technical aspects.

Local governments may conduct at-home interviews by mail, telephone, or by an in-person interview. Of these, the mail survey is the least expensive method but also the least accurate. The in-person survey is the most expensive and probably the most accurate method. The telephone survey may be a good compromise — at least in areas where most households have telephones. The problem of unlisted numbers is being reduced by random dialing techniques. The use of this technique by local governments is being tested in a number of cities.

The cost of surveys is closely related to the number of

interviews. The cost-precision trade-off from increasing the sample size is discussed further in Reference 60. If a jurisdiction happens to be undertaking an origin-destination survey, further questions for effectiveness measurement could be included at little additional cost. Similarly, it is economical to combine surveys that encompass a number of crucial services (trash service, recreation, and law enforcement, for examples) as well as transportation.

The accuracy of survey results is influenced by such considerations as the wording of questions, the memory of respondents, the size and method of selecting the sample, the ability to locate respondents, and the willingness of citizens to respond. To permit comparisons of a rough but sufficient degree of precision among neighborhoods or service areas, a sample size of about 100 interviews per area is probably adequate. This implies about 600 interviews in a jurisdiction with six such areas. [22] The number of interviews may necessarily be greater where data is to be disaggre-

22. With these small sample sizes, small differences from year to year of, say, plus or minus three or four percentage points would not be significant at the 90 percent confidence level. For example, if 9 percent of the respondents rated their overall satisfaction with the transportation in their city as "poor" in one year, and 11 percent in the next year, the difference of two percentage points then would reveal a greater than 10 percent probability that this difference occurred merely because of the sample selection rather than because there was a change in the satisfaction level of the citizens in the city. For comparing samples of about 100 respondents, even differences of five percentage points have a nontrivial possibility of being due to sample selection. Nevertheless, if used with caution, we feel that this precision is sufficient for reasonable uses of the information—recognizing that government decision making is generally made under conditions of considerably greater uncertainty. The cost savings from not going to much larger samples (which would increase the precision), we believe, are too important to suggest much larger annual surveys.

gated by many population subgroups. Before drawing the sample, the categories by which data will be disaggregated should be determined to insure that a sufficient number of persons or interviews are collected from each category.

The types of questions that could be included in such a survey are illustrated in the Appendix. Prior to administering the survey, the questionnaire should be properly tested to insure that question wording is understandable and that it produces required data. Questions 8-11 of the Appendix are intended to provide an estimate of overall citizen satisfaction with local transportation services. The percentage of citizens analyzed who respond in a certain way would be used as the measure of overall satisfaction, e.g., percent of respondents who respond that their overall satisfaction with the transportation in the city is "excellent" or "good" rather than "fair" or "poor" (see Question 8 of the Appendix).

Data from the survey could be collated according to various personal characteristics of respondents to the survey. Such factors as the number of automobiles owned, the availability of automobiles for personal use, and the age, sex, handicap, or residential location of the respondent can be ascertained in the survey. Separating survey responses according to such personal characteristics may reveal deficiencies of transportation service to certain population groups.

The survey might also be used to provide information on how citizens value various aspects of transportation services— if appropriate questions are added to the survey.

V. Clientele Groupings

Certain segments of the urban population may have different needs for service transportation or may be receiving different quality service than other segments. For instance, a high proportion of young and elderly residents of urban areas may lack access to personal automobiles. Members of this group rely upon public transit modes more heavily than other groups. Residents of some neighborhoods may be relatively isolated from other areas because transit service is not available to them when needed or does not connect with desired destinations. Therefore, any analysis of the effectiveness of a local transportation system should consider how well the needs of such subgroups are being met.

By analyzing measurement data separated by subgroups, weaknesses in transportation service can be identified. Once identified, weaknesses may suggest relatively inexpensive remedies such as changes in service schedules or routing. Where more elaborate changes in the transportation system are necessary to meet subgroup needs, measurement data will better enable policy officials to evaluate the potential impact of each proposed remedy upon the subgroup's mobility. Some policy alternatives might increase mobility of a population subgroup at some sacrifice to the effectiveness of transportation services on the area as a whole. In evaluating such trade-offs it is especially important to be able to compare effects upon each population group as explicitly as possible.

Some of the important subgroups for which transportation measurement data might be separately analyzed are:

- Persons not having regular access to an automobile (including families not owning an automobile, youths below driving age but old enough to use public transit independently, adults unable or unwilling to drive, and other family members without regular access to an automobile at certain hours of the day).

- Age groups, especially the young and elderly.

- Low income groups.

- Full-time employees, secondary workers (part-time), and nonworkers.

- Racial or ethnic groups.

- Persons with a physical handicap.

- Geographical or neighborhood areas.

Wherever possible, data on each measure should be collected in a form which allows disaggregation into these socioeconomic and geographical subgroups.[1]

To some extent the size and location of the subgroups listed above can be identified from census data by block or tract. Automobile ownership, age distribution, income level, employment status of the household members, and physical disability were gathered by tract in the 1970 Census.

The least costly method for applying measures by sub-

---

1. Data on Measures 1, 2, 6, 9, and 12 are especially useful when disaggregated by users of public and private modes, or many socioeconomic groups. Measures 4, 10, and 11 pertain directly to routes or corridors of travel and the adjacent geographical areas. Procedures for collecting data in a manner which allows such disaggregation is discussed in Chapter IV.

group is to identify census blocks or tracts where high proportions of each subgroup reside. Then measurement data from these areas can be scrutinized to determine the level of service these areas are receiving and whether the type of service (such as the mix of modes) is appropriate to the particular needs of the subgroup. In some cases, a subgroup may be concentrated at a particular point (such as convalescent hospital or old age home) or members may frequently travel to particular points (teenage recreation center). Service to and from such points may also warrant special consideration of the adequacy of service to the subgroup.

Neighborhoods

Geographic subunit is perhaps the most significant division by which data can be analyzed. Different areas or jurisdictions are likely to have different transportation needs (by virtue of their density, predominant land use, distance from services, and, socioeconomic characteristics) and service available. To analyze the effectiveness of the transportation system by geographic area, the jurisdiction should be divided into relatively homogeneous subsections or neighborhoods. The size of each might vary roughly between half a square mile and five square miles. To delineate neighborhoods local officials can refer to physical and socioeconomic characteristics of the urban area as identified by visual inspections, census data, discussion with government personnel and residents, and highway and transit line routes. Each service area preferably would be defined by its predominant socioeconomic characteristics and requirements for transportation services. Many local governments have established neighborhood areas for analysis of other municipal services. The geographical subunits for transportation service analysis might be drawn to coincide with these districts. Exhibit 6 illustrates how a city might be divided into neighborhood districts. Exhibit 2 showed

Exhibit 6. ILLUSTRATIVE CITY NEIGHBORHOOD DIVISIONS

City Limits

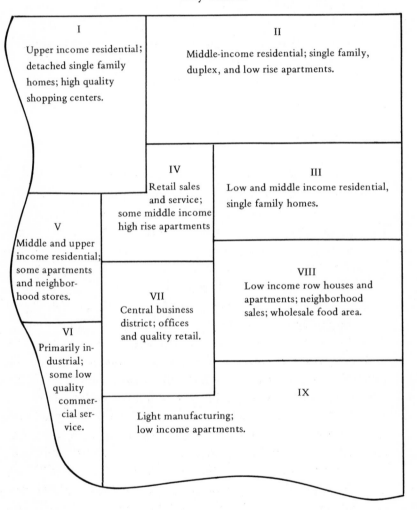

I
Upper income residential; detached single family homes; high quality shopping centers.

II
Middle-income residential; single family, duplex, and low rise apartments.

IV
Retail sales and service; some middle income high rise apartments

III
Low and middle income residential, single family homes.

V
Middle and upper income residential; some apartments and neighborhood stores.

VII
Central business district; offices and quality retail.

VIII
Low income row houses and apartments; neighborhood sales; wholesale food area.

VI
Primarily industrial; some low quality commercial service.

IX
Light manufacturing; low income apartments.

City Limits

how such data might be summarized and presented by neighborhood.

Data on accessibility and convenience (Measures 1 and 2), travel time (Measure 3), road surface quality (Measure 5), safety (Measures 7 and 8), and overall citizen perception of service adequacy (Measure 12) particularly merit disaggregation by neighborhood.

Automobile Ownership

Auto ownership is an especially relevant factor when measuring accessibility and convenience (Measures 1 and 2), travel time (Measure 3), and overall citizen perception of service adequacy (Measure 12). Analysis should not only include consideration of households not owning an automobile but also households with members below driving age or with family members who lack access to automobiles at all or certain times of the day (perhaps because their family has only one car). Data on the number of automobiles owned per household can be obtained from census data by tract and from state and local automobile registration information. A household may own an automobile, but it may be unavailable to most members during a large part of the week, forcing them to rely on a public mode. A common example of this is a household where one member uses the family automobile for commuting to work, leaving other adult members of the household without private means of travel during work hours. We suggest that data on ownership be supplemented with information on automobile availability gathered by citizen survey. Some local governments may also be able to draw upon local transportation model data to identify areas of low auto ownership or areas where persons might prefer to use a public mode should service be made available.

Data for some measures will pertain more directly to comparisons by travel route, rather than by neighborhood. Measures 3, 4, 7, 9, 10, and 11 become especially useful when classified according to travel link or route.

VI. Recommendations and Cost Estimates For a Basic Measurement System

General Recommendations

1. The effectiveness of current local transportation services and the potential impact of proposals on citizens of the community should be evaluated using measures such as those listed in Chapter III.

2. Regular collection of data on the measures should be undertaken to permit at least an annual evaluation of local transportation services as they affect the public.

3. Staff time, effort, and money are required for properly collecting and collating the recommended data. Therefore such effectiveness evaluation should be undertaken only if the local government intends to analyze the information and utilize it in making decisions. The measurements in this report are suggested to complement data collection and analysis presently used for transportation planning in the community.

Specific Suggestions for Data Collection

1. Probably the greatest gap in current transportation data is information to evaluate accessibility and convenience. Therefore, we suggest that first priority be given to analysis of citizen proximity to public transit stops and to finding out where key trip times are greater than one hour (Measure 1).

2. Key concentrations of community employment, commerce, and recreation activities should be identified and travel times regularly measured between them and residential neighborhoods (Measure 3).

3. A periodic citizen survey should be conducted at least

annually to assess citizen satisfaction on convenience, comfort, and overall satisfaction (Measures 2, 6, and 12). This could be supplemented by an annual on-board survey of public transit users. Sampling should be used to reduce the costs, but with sound statistical methods to maintain the representativeness of the results.

4. Available statistics on traffic accidents and local transportation-related air and noise pollution should be tabulated according to categories that relate to local government objectives in planning and improving the transportation system.

5. Data should be disaggregated by neighborhood and relevant population groups as described in Chapter V so that the levels of services and relative needs of such groups can be considered.

Cost of Data Collection and Analysis

Exhibit 7 shows estimates of the cost of a continuing program of field measurement and analysis encompassing the measures of effectiveness suggested in this study. An incremental approach in reaching this level of effort is desirable to assure proper utilization of such capacity.

As shown in Exhibit 7, the estimated staffing requirements range from approximately three man-years for jurisdictions of about 150,000 population to about six and one-half man-years for those of about 750,000. Many of the tasks included probably could be performed by personnel presently assigned to the traffic division or another agency of the government. Some of the additional costs of data collection might be absorbed by reprogramming existing monies or redefining certain existing jobs.

Exhibit 7. ESTIMATED ANNUAL COST FOR A
CONTINUOUS PROGRAM FOR DATA
COLLECTION AND ANALYSIS [a]

	Typical City Size		
	750,000	300,000	150,000
Average City Area (in square miles)	60	45	35
Personnel Requirements (in man-years)			
Field Measurements	3	2	1.5
Clerical	1.5	1	.5
Analysis	2	1.5	1
Total	6.5	4.5	3
Annual Costs (in dollars) [b]			
Field measurements	$39,000	$24,000	$16,500
Clerical	12,000	7,000	3,000
Program analysis	30,000	21,000	12,000
Citizen attitude survey [c]	12,000	7,500	6,000
Total annual costs for data collection, evaluation and analysis	$93,000	$59,500	$37,500

a. These rough estimates represent the added costs over present likely allocations for traffic surveys and statistical efforts by typical cities. To the extent that existing personnel can be utilized for the additional tasks the costs listed above would be reduced proportionately. Perhaps as much as one-half of this effort could be absorbed by existing personnel in many local governments.

b. Costs for each inspector are estimated to be $13,000, $12,000, and $11,000 respectively for the three city sizes; for clerical workers — $8,000, $7,000 and $6,000 respectively (including benefits); for analysts — $15,000, $14,000 and $12,000 respectively (including benefits and data processing costs).

c. Costs based on Reference 59, assuming that the three city (or county) sizes would carry out 900, 600, and 500 interviews respectively.

A city may find shortcuts to some data gathering, as when air and noise pollution are monitored and measured by another local agency. Also, public transit firms might be persuaded to assist in surveying their clients, especially if questions included in the survey could help the company plan transit service. Inspection and clerical staff requirements would be reduced in proportion to the number of such opportunities for shared data collection resources.

A metropolitan transportation planning agency is another major source of resources and possibly data. It may also be possible for the transportation attitude surveys to be combined with surveys (if undertaken regularly) regarding other functional areas, thereby substantially reducing the special effort required.[1]

Many potential sources of funds other than local government revenues may be tapped for these purposes. Federal funds that may be used for some of the data collection and analysis include grants from the Urban Mass Transportation Administration, the Department of Housing and Urban Development "701" General Planning Assistance, and the Community Development Programs. These grants usually require one-third to one-half matching funds from the local jurisdiction.

---

1. Such combined citizen surveys are discussed in Reference 58.

Appendix

Illustrative Types of Questions for Citizen Survey of Local Transportation Service Quality[1]

The particular measures of effectiveness (M/E) most relevant to each type of question are shown in parentheses; the M/E numbers refer back to Exhibit 1 and to Chapter IV where each is described.

A. <u>Questions on Background of Responding Households</u>

    1.   Number of automobiles owned?

    2.   Income class?

    3.   Age of respondent?

    4.   Sex of respondent?

    5.   Size and composition of family?

    6.   Number in family with fulltime or part-time employment?

    7.   Frequency of use of public transit and of automobile for various types of typical trips within the city or county: e.g., about daily, about once a week, about once a month, less than once a month?

---

1. The wording used here is for illustrative purposes only; the questions have not been tested or placed in questionnaire format. In an actual survey, the wording of questions of these types should be carefully formulated and tested to make certain they are understandable and provide data required as the basis for decision making.

B.   Overall Quality of Transportation Services

(M/E 12)   8.   How would you rate your overall satisfaction
                   with the transportation in this city (county):
                   excellent, good, fair, or poor?

(M/E 12)   9.   As compared to last year have transportation
                   services been getting better, worse, or are they
                   about the same?

(M/E 12)   10.   How would you rate your overall satisfaction
                   with public transit within the city (county):
                   excellent, good, fair, or poor?

(M/E 12)   11.   How would you rate your overall satisfaction
                   with automobile driving conditions within the
                   city (county): excellent, good, fair, or poor?

(M/E 1   12.   Thinking of all types of trips (work, recreation,
and 2)   shopping, etc.), how would you rate your over-
                   all ability to get to the places you want to go
                   within this city (county): excellent, good, fair,
                   or poor?

C.   Specific Issues on Public Transit (These issues should be
     included in questions asked of non-users of public transit
     as well as users.)

            13.   How would you rate the transit vehicles in
                   this city (county) on the following comfort
                   factors:

M/E 6)   a)   Temperature/humidity: usually comfor-
                         table, occasionally uncomfortable, often

uncomfortable, usually uncomfortable?

(M/E 6) b) Crowdedness: almost always get a seat; occasionally have to stand at least part of the way; almost always have to stand most of the trip.

(M/E 6) c) Noisiness: quiet, mostly quiet, fairly noisy, very noisy?

(M/E 6) d) Cleanliness: clean, mostly clean, fairly dirty, very dirty?

(M/E 6) e) Courteousness of drivers: usually very courteous, fairly courteous, unpleasant?

(M/E 6) f) Odors: no problem, occasional bothersome fumes or odors, usually unpleasant?

14. How would you rate the transit system in this city (county) on the following convenience factors:

(M/E 2) a) Nearness of a transit stop to home: none close enough for use, long walk, fairly close by?

(M/E 2) b) Routes: do not go to most places where I would want to go; too much time or too many transfers to go to most places where I would want to go; some I can get to conveniently – some I can't; routes go to most places where I want to go within the city (county).

(M/E 2)   c)   Frequency during peak hours: not nearly frequent enough, fair, satisfactory?

(M/E 2)   d)   Frequency during off-peak hours: not nearly frequent enough, fair, satisfactory?

(M/E 2)   e)   Information on rates and schedules: information very difficult to get, can be obtained with a little effort, readily available?

(M/E 2)   f)   Frequency of missed schedules: frequently schedules are badly missed, occasionally missed schedules, usually on or close to schedule?

15.   For non-users of public transit: How would you rate each of the following factors as a reason that you have not used public transit for travel within this city (county):

		Major Reason	Minor Reason	Not a Reason
(M/E 2)	a) Takes too long			
(M/E 2)	b) Transit stop not close enough			
(M/E 2)	c) Transit runs too infrequently			
(M/E 2)	d) Routes do not go to desired destination			
(M/E 2)	e) Prefer convenience of automobile			

			Major Reason	Minor Reason	Not a Reason
(M/E 6)	f)	Transit vehicles too uncomfortable and unpleasant			
(M/E 6)	g)	Too crowded			
(M/E 8)	h)	Too dangerous			
(M/E 9)	i)	Too expensive			
	j)	Other (Specify)			

16. How would you rate each of the following factors as to reasons for your non-use of automobiles for travel within the city (county):

			Major Reason	Minor Reason	Not a Reason
(M/E 1)	a)	Don't have access to automobile			
(M/E 9)	b)	Too expensive			
(M/E 6)	c)	Too much traffic			
(M/E 6)	d)	Don't like traveling in an automobile			
(M/E 1)	e)1	Can't drive; too old/young/infirm to drive			
	f)	Other (Specify)			

D. Special Issues on Automobile Travel

(M/E 2)   17.   How difficult is it usually to find parking at your destination (peak/off-peak): many places available, few places available, usually have to search for a space?

(M/E 2)   18.   How would you rate the quality of street identification signs and traffic signs and signals: satisfactory, occasionally difficult to understand, often difficult to understand, usually difficult to understand?

(M/E 5   19.   How would you rate the quality of the road
and 6)   surfaces over which you ride within this city (county): generally smooth, occasionally bumpy, frequently bumpy, very bumpy?

E.   Environmental Noise

(M/E 10)   20.   To what extent have you been bothered either at home or at work by noise from motor vehicles during the past month: not at all, on a few occasions, often, often and with considerable annoyance?

F.   Travel Time Information

The survey can also be used to obtain information on estimated walking time to transit stops or to parking at both ends of the trip, transit waiting times, and travel time (whether by transit or automobile). The responses, however, may suffer from the inaccuracy or memory limitations of those questioned. If combined with information on specific origins and destinations, total trip times can be related to distance traveled.

References

1. Alan M. Voorhees and Associates, Inc., <u>A Systems Analysis of Transit Routes and Schedules</u>, prepared for Washington Metropolitan Area Transit Commission, November 1969.

2. American Association of State Highway Officials, National Association of Counties, and National League of Cities, <u>Highways and Urban Development</u>, Report on Second National Conference, 1965.

3. American Association of State Highway Officials, <u>Road Use Benefit Analyses for Highway Improvements</u>, 1960.

4. Appleyard, Mark and Mark Lintell, "Environmental Quality of City Streets," Working Paper 142, Center for Planning and Development Research, University of California (Berkeley), December 1970.

5. Bolt, Beranek, and Newman, Inc., <u>Noise in Urban and Suburban Areas</u>, January 1967.

6. Boots, Andrew J., III, et al, <u>Inequality in Local Government Services: A Case Study of Neighborhood Roads</u>, The Urban Institute, 1972.

7. Boyce, David E., <u>The Role of Urban Development Models in the Planmaking Process</u>, Philadelphia, June 1969.

8. Brown, Albert and Ronald T. Kirby, <u>Measuring Urban Performance</u>, Working Paper 708-57, The Urban Institute, November 1971.

9. Bureau of Public Roads, <u>Conducting a Comprehensive Parking Study</u>, Procedure Manual, 1957.

77

10. _____, Conducting a Limited
    Parking Study, 1957.

11. _____, Manual of Procedures
    for Metropolitan Area Traffic Studies, 1946.

12. Cary, W. N. Jr. and P. E. Irich, "The Pavement Service-
    ability-Performance Concept, " Highway Research
    Board, Bulletin 250, 1960.

13. Crumlish, Joseph D., Notes on the State of the Art of
    Benefit Cost Analysis as Related to Transporta-
    tion Systems, Technical Note 294, National
    Bureau of Standards, U.S. Department of
    Commerce, November 1966.

14. Ellis, Raymond H. and Richard D. Worrall, Toward
    Measurement of Community Impact: the Util-
    ization of Longitudinal Travel Data to Define
    Residential Linkages (unpublished), Highway
    Research Board, Highway Research Record 277,
    January 1969.

15. Fagin, Henry, "Urban Transportation Criteria," The
    Annals of the Academy of Political and Social
    Sciences, Vol. 352, March 1964.

16. Galloway, William J., Welden E. Clark, and Jean Kerrick,
    Highway Noise Simulation and Mixed Reaction,
    Highway Research Board, Program Report 78,
    1969.

17. Glass, David C. and Jerome E. Singer, "Behavior After-
    effects of Unpredictable and Uncontrollable
    Aversive Events," American Scientist, Vol. 60
    No. 4, July-August 1972.

18. Grecco, W. L. and S. M. Breuning, "A Systems Engineering Model for Trip Generation and Distribution," Travel Forecasting, Highway Research Board, Highway Research Record 38, 1963.

19. Hatry, Harry P., Criteria for Evaluation of Planning State and Local Programs, Subcommittee on Intergovernmental Relations, United States Senate, July 1967.

20. Hauser, Edwin W., Leonard L. West, and A. Richard Schlercher, "Fundamental Air Pollution Considerations for Urban and Transportation Planners," Traffic Quarterly, January 1972.

21. Highway Research Board, Community Consequences of Highway Development, Program Report 18, 1965.

22. _____ , Comparison of Different Methods of Measuring Pavement Condition: Interim Report, Program Report 7, 1964.

23. _____ , Highway Capacity Manual, Special Report 87, 1965.

24. _____ , Origin and Destination Surveys, Methods, and Costs, Bulletin 76, 1953.

25. _____ , Running Costs of Vehicles as Affected by Road Design and Traffic, Program Report, 1971.

26. _____ , Urban Land Use Concepts and Models, Highway Research Record 207, 1967.

80

27. _____ , <u>Transportation and Community</u>
<u>Values,</u> Special Report 105, 1969.

28. _____ , <u>Transportation System Analysis</u>
<u>and Evaluation of Alternate Plans</u>, Highway
Research Record 180, 1967.

29. _____ , <u>Transportation System Evalua-</u>
<u>tion,</u> Highway Research Record 238, 1968.

30. _____ , <u>Urban Development Models,</u>
Special Report 97, 1968.

31. _____ , <u>Use of Census Data in Urban</u>
<u>Planning,</u> Special Report 121, 1970.

32. "Initial Progress Report on 'Improved Methods for Estimating Transportation Effects' Project," Working
Paper 450-1, The Urban Institute, May 1969.

33. Kemp, Michael A., <u>Some Evidence of Transit Demand</u>
<u>Elasticities</u>, Working Paper 708-52, The Urban
Institute, November 1971.

34. Kentucky Department of Highways, Highway Research
Laboratory, <u>Pavement Roughness Studies,</u>
April 1962.

35. Klein, George E., "Evaluation of New Transportation
Systems," <u>Defining Transportation Requirements,</u>
American Society of Mechanical Engineering,
1968.

36. Lansing, John B. and Gary Hendricks, <u>Automobile</u>

Ownership and Residential Density, Institute for Social Research, University of Michigan, June 1967.

37. Leavitt, Helen, "The Rotting of Our Air," Potomac Magazine, The Washington Post, December 19, 1971

38. Meyer, J. N., J. F. Kain, and Martin Wohl, The Urban Transportation Problem, Cambridge, Mass.: Harvard University Press, 1971.

39. Moser, Patricia J., "Aesthetic and Ecological Disharmonies of Highways," Transportation, Vol. 1 No. 1, May 1972.

40. Nahammura, V. F., "Serviceability Ratings of Highway Pavements," Pavement Condition Evaluation, Highway Research Board, Report 7, 1964.

41. Organization for Economic Cooperation and Development, Urban Transportation Noise, Report of the Consultative Group on Transportation Research, 1971.

42. Orange County, California, "Objectives and Effectiveness Factors for Budget Structures" (Program IV and VII), June 30, 1972.

43. Pardee, E. S., et al, Measurement and Evaluation of Transportation System Effectiveness, The RAND Corporation, Santa Monica, California, September 1969.

44. Peterson, Arnold P. and Kevin E. Gross, Handbook of Noise Measurement, General Radio Company, 1967.

45. Public Administration Service, Measuring Transit Service, Procedure Manual, 1958.

46. _____ , Recommended Standards, Warrants and Objectives for Transit Services and Facilities, Procedure Manual, 1958.

47. Robinson, D. W., The Concept of Noise Pollution Level, Report AC38, National Physical Laboratory, Aerodynamics Division, United Kingdom, March 1969.

48. Seidman, David R., The Construction of an Urban Growth Model, Delaware Valley Regional Planning Commission, Report 1.

49. Serendipity, Inc., A Study of the Magnitude of Transportation and Potential Abatement, November 1967, (Prepared for Office of Noise Abatement, Arlington, Va.)

50. Starr, Edward A., "Measuring Noise Pollution," Spectrum, Institute of Electrical and Electronics Engineering, June 1972.

51. State Highway Commission, State of Wisconsin, Highways I: The Basis for Planning, 1967.

52. Texas Department of Highways, A Comparison of Four Roughness Measuring Systems, June 1969.

53. U. S. Department of Health, Education, and Welfare, Public Health Service, "Calculating Future Carbon Monoxide Emissions and Concentrations from Urban Traffic Data," June 1967.

54. U. S. Department of Transportation, "Draft Impact State-